Muck Boots,

Sticky Notes,

God

And

Me!

Muck Boots,

Sticky Notes,

God

And

Me !

Written and Illustrated by

Amber Dobson Woodrum

PREPARING THE WAY

PUBLISHERS

**PREPARING
THE WAY
PUBLISHERS
411 Zandecki Road
Chehalis, WA   98532 USA**

**Amber Dobson Woodrum
Muck Boots, Sticky Notes, God and Me!**

ISBN-13: 978-0615441948   ISBN-10: 0615441947

Printed in the United States of America

DEDICATIONS

This book is dedicated to:

MY HUSBAND, for loving me enough to actually read this book; and not just "skim it." You are so easy to draw inspiration from...

MY CHILDREN, who think I'm a *ROCKSTAR!* You may think that you're MY biggest fans, but it's ME that's star-struck by the four of you...

~~~~~~~

ACKNOWLEDGMENTS

A special thanks to my next door neighbors, who happen to be my parents. Daddy Dave and Momma Jan, I could not have done this without your love, support and enthusiasm! Thanks for taking time out of your busy lives to help me put this project together. I'm crazy about living life with YOU!

CONTENTS

Introduction

I'd like to think that I am not a complicated person. I lead a simple, yet fulfilling life as a wife, mother, home-school teacher, "sports junkie" and now author. I love drawing with pastels and dabble in photography from time to time. Simple enough!

My children are always telling me that I should *"be on Oprah..."* I assumed they were referencing some aspect of my personality that they thought was just *too good for the world to miss out on!* After all, they are my biggest fans! It wasn't until recently that I realized my children's desire to see me appear on *"Oprah"* had nothing to do with my personality at all. "You're complicated, Mom. Complicated stories always end up on *Oprah*."

I must admit that my children have experienced a vast array of complicated emotions, which seem to *"OOZE"* out of me when the sticky situations of life come my way. It's these very sticky situations in life that have qualified me for *"The Oprah Winfrey Show"* in their opinions.

However, I'd like to believe that I am not unlike YOU. We are fairly regular people, leading fairly regular lives; but we've had to endure a fairly complicated story or two (or three or four...) in life.

None of the complicated stories in my life have made news headlines or warranted a public appearance of any sort, and maybe yours haven't either; but that doesn't mean they aren't REAL. You know what complicated stories I'm talking about: *abuse, neglect, death, suicide, unemployment, homelessness, separation, divorce, depression, debt, drugs...*the list could go on forever; and the vast array of emotions that accompany stories like these seem to only complicate things further. When my children referred to my own complicated stories, they were referring to some of the very things I've listed above.

As I pondered the idea of appearing on national television to tell the world of the stories that have made this rather simple girl so complicated, I began comparing my more heart-breaking tales with ones I've seen on TV programs similar to *"The Oprah Winfrey Show."* How they compare makes no difference. The heartbreak is real for all of us and the trials of life can add up to tell a very sad story.

That brings us to the purpose of this book. The 'sad stories' of my life began to puddle up on me; hence the need for MUCK BOOTS in the title. I began to feel what I think are the normal emotions one would expect to be feeling during times of struggle: confusion, hopelessness, pain, sorrow, and anger; as well as a myriad of other ones. As I began to harbor these different feelings deep within my heart, my mind, and my soul, I began to lose the ability to see clearly. It was as if I was blinded by the rains that were pouring down from what we would call ***the storms of life.***

Quoting the words of David in the Bible, Psalm 40:12 says, *"For troubles without number surround me; my sins have overtaken me and I cannot see..."* It became completely difficult to fix my gaze on anything besides my sad stories. I even lost sight of God.

Looking ahead into the pages of this book, however, you will NOT find my sad stories written out in detail for you to read. What you WILL discover is how the Lord moved me from simply *coping* with the pain and confusion of my circumstances, to *conquering* my own sin and muddied thoughts; exchanging them for a new way of thinking...a way of thinking that lines up with the mind and truth of Christ.

Let us begin our journey together with this particular truth in mind:

"He will wipe every tear from their eyes, and there will be no more death or sorrow or crying or pain. All these things are gone forever." And the one sitting on the throne said, "Look, I am making everything new..."

Revelation 21:4-5 NLT

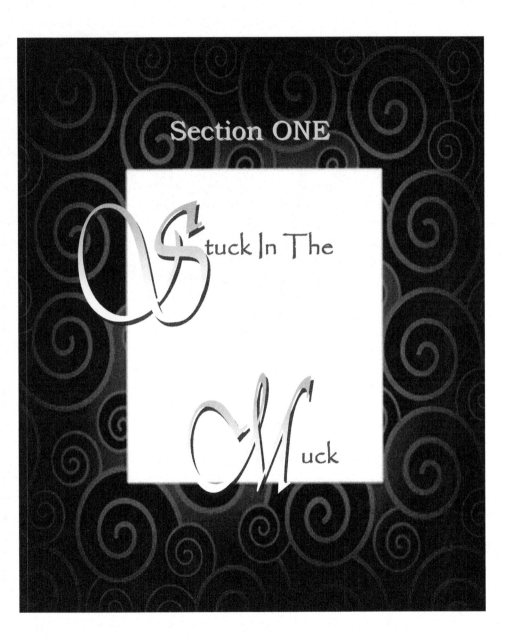

Section ONE

Stuck In The Muck

1

My Muck Boots

"Jerry, let's not share our sad stories." I woke this morning recalling this line from the 1996 blockbuster film "*Jerry Maguire.*" (1996, TriStar Films). I could literally see the actress Renee Zellweger sitting across from actor Tom Cruise, leaning in just slightly, and whispering these seemingly enlightened words. I pondered them only briefly and was quickened to remember something similar that the Lord spoke to my heart only a year ago. I was sitting in church on a Sunday morning and *again* reliving the pains of my life. Let's be honest, we all have our own "sad stories." I was not only mucking around in them; I had sunk to wallowing in mine! The Lord spoke to my heart, saying, "You have exalted your position as *victim* over My position as *VICTOR* for far too long." It hit me like a ton of bricks. He was right. I had been dwelling on my sad stories, mulling over my victimizations in life so much that I couldn't even see my God, my victorious King through all the *muck.*

I began to realize that I kept needing Jesus to be my Savior, but had never allowed myself to walk in the victory of *what* He has saved me from. This has been a continuing theme that I have had to revisit all too often, and this is one of those times.

For the last year, my family has faced some tremendous challenges spiritually which have been accompanied by physical hardships as well.

We have had leading and direction from the Lord regarding these situations, followed by appropriate confirmation to back it up...or so it seemed. Recently, however, circumstances have gotten even more challenging, and suddenly those things we had been hoping in, trusting God for, and believing Him to do have happened quite opposite of what we had expected. Talk about a bulldozer! It has chased me down, run me over and buried me in this muck I speak of.

The other day, I realized that it was as if I had, at some point, gone shopping and bought myself "muck boots" and put them on with the intention of just standing there in the muck! There I was wallowing in it, getting more and more comfortable...wondering why God wouldn't speak, help, fix, move, or DO something! I even began questioning whether my entire walk with Him had been a lie. Oh yes, this muck was thick! There I stood, in the middle of this mud puddle

mess and looking straight ahead... but not knowing where to go. I had all these choices in front of me and no direction from the Lord. The pain, hurt and disappointment I was feeling seemed to be blinding me to any amount of truth within me. I had such deep confusion about who I was to God, and who God was to me. This kaleidoscope of emotions had surfaced only a short time ago.

Finally, this morning, I know what I have to do. Awakened by the famous line from the aforementioned blockbuster film playing in my mind...followed by a quickening of my spirit to remember the words of the Lord to my heart, I can no longer "exalt my position as *victim* over HIS position as VICTOR" in my life.

This decision I made to put on my muck boots and stand in my puddle was never a long-term resolve. I may not know looking forward, which

step out of the puddle will provide the firmest footing for me. I don't know the future, and I have no clear direction from the Lord which way to go.

In light of these facts, I turn around and I look instead at the path behind me. There lies the long road the Lord and I have journeyed together to get to this point. There were mud puddles there, as well...ones that I stood in for much too long, and ones I would rather never fall into again. Yet, today, as I look back again down this lane; I don't see the mud puddles; I see a smoothly paved road. I see clearly, without the rains of pain and confusion clouding my vision. See, the storms have already been weathered there. The muck has dried up under the influence of the sun...or should I say, SON. Those were muddy places where I once stood as a victim, much like I stand in today. But looking back, I see that I didn't just get out of the muck by myself and move forward. All along the way God has been repaving my road. I am not simply looking down a path of past pain...I'm gazing upon my very own VICTORY LANE.

I may not know where I'm headed, but there's an amazing testimony of where I've been...and it feels like just the right time to take a long walk.

"I remember the days of old. I ponder all your great works and think about what you have done."
Psalm 143:5

2

Back to Victory Lane

Again I hear the line "Jerry, let's not share our sad stories." This is exactly my plan...I don't need to recall again the pain I have been saved from. I need to remember the One who saved me. This journey I'm preparing to take is down my very own Victory Lane. Not that I have arrived anywhere! (Remember, I am going backwards at this point.) However, if I don't make this trip back to see the evidences of the Lord's gracious and loving interventions in my life, I don't know that I will have the strength to move forward in faith...out of the puddle in which I now stand.   In essence, this is simply exercise for me. Yes, I **AM** going to take a walk into the testimonies God has blessed my life with up to this point in order to *exercise* my faith.

3

Finding Sticky Notes

"The faithful love of the LORD never ends!
His mercies never cease.
Great is his faithfulness;
his mercies begin afresh each morning.
I say to myself, "The LORD is my inheritance;
therefore, I will hope in him!"
Lamentations 3:22-24 NLT

I remember writing this scripture down on a sticky note one day, and I stuck it somewhere around the house in plain sight so that it would serve as a reminder to me. And now, as I revisit the testimonies of the Lord in and around my life, I am really reminding myself of His faithfulness! No matter how obvious, sometimes I need a reminder!

Just the other day, I remember walking out to my car to take my daughter to school. I noticed that my rear tire was nearly flat. I knew

in my mind that I needed to put air in my tire before driving down the road or I'd be stranded. I proceeded to load all four of my children, my dog, our bags, my car keys, my (indispensible) coffee mug and then myself into the car. I started it up and drove off! It wasn't until I was sitting at a stop light (when a kind gentleman who was driving behind me ran up to my window to alert me of a nearly-flat tire) that I had even remembered I needed air. Not even 10 minutes of time had elapsed since I left home, and already I needed a sticky note to remind me!

I don't know about you, but no matter the brand of sticky note I buy, they all tend to lose their stickiness after a while. Occasionally, I will move a large piece of furniture that hasn't been moved for some time and I will find an old sticky note lying underneath it. It's always interesting to read what is jotted down, and try to remember the situations that prompted the sticky notes in the first place.

Well, it's time to rearrange some things again. I am not talking about physical furniture in my house...but I am talking about some pretty significant pieces in my mind and in my heart. Some pieces are broken and in need of major repair. Some pieces simply need dusting off. There are even pieces that only need to be moved so that I have a different perspective or point-of-view. No longer can I sit in the dusty corners of my mind wondering where my God is. I am going to start turning things over, looking for those lost reminders...those sticky notes that take me back to those times when God demonstrated His faithfulness clearly.

It's so easy to dream about remodeling. Magazines and Do-it-Yourself programs lend themselves nicely to lofty ideals. Of course, in reality you must have the resources necessary to accomplish the task at hand. But as I take a self inventory it seems I have no resources left. There is going to be NO moving forward until I get some. I will have to work with what I have.

What I have is my sad stories hung on the walls of my heart, and a pile of sticky notes in my hands...

It's time to redecorate. Let's read some of them, and together we can see where they fit into the paisley-print of my new décor.

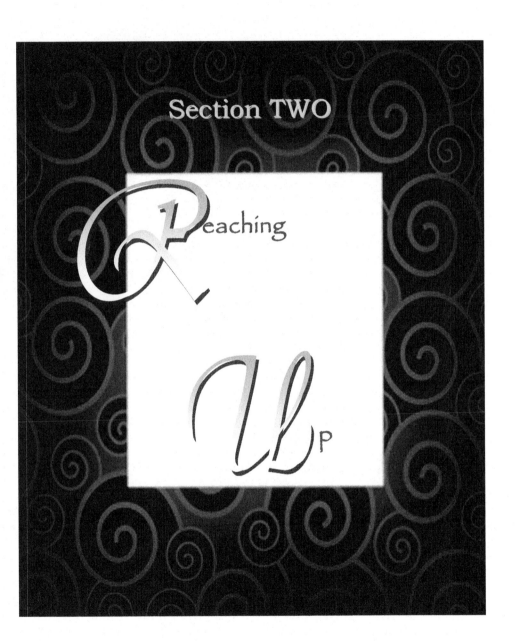

Section TWO

Reaching Up

4

Learning to Love

"If you've given your first love away...then you can love him like nobody can..."

These were the words to the song playing in the cassette player of my green 1999 Oldsmobile Alero the night I drove back home to my husband after five weeks of separation. Consequently, it's the night I also came to the Lord. The words as belted out by Wayne Watson only added fuel to the fire I was feeling inside my heart as I nervously fumbled with the car keys. I couldn't get them into the ignition fast enough. It was the longest five-mile drive back to the duplex where we had shared a life for the last four years. I had moved out and left my husband and two small children for many reasons. Those make up some of my "sad stories." But what I want to talk about is how I moved back in...

At this point, I would normally begin to tell you how terribly bad things had gotten in my marriage. I would go into great detail, and probably catch myself in an exaggeration or two, in an attempt to portray the marital PIT from which the Lord pulled us. But, I don't want to go there. I want to go to that moment the Lord gave my heart a chance for change. I was sitting in my bedroom in the little apartment I had rented for myself. It was nearly two o'clock in the morning and I just couldn't seem to escape my own thoughts. (Strange as it seems, when I look back at myself, it was really as if I had a "good" version of myself on one shoulder and an "evil" version of myself on the other. Just like you would see in the cartoons, both of these versions of myself were talking AT me nonstop.) I was literally going through every choice I had made, every conversation I'd had and every conversation I did not have during the last five weeks of our separation. I was weighing them. I was agonizing over things that I didn't even fully understand. I remember clearly sitting on my bed with my Bible next to me. Somehow, I knew reading the Bible was "the right thing to do." I would pick it up and read some of it only to toss it back down because it felt foreign to me...even generic. Certainly there was no God audibly speaking to me through the scriptures on the page! I remember desperately wanting to have this big experience where God or an angel would come into my room. At that moment he would tell me that if I didn't turn from my sin to serve God, then I would live eternally in fiery damnation. You see, I had some knowledge of the Bible and I had accepted Jesus as a small child. I was never in disbelief that God or His Son, Jesus, existed. I just had never walked in fellowship or relationship with God, Jesus or the Holy Spirit.

I wanted God to come to me supernaturally and threaten me with Hell. I would be forced to choose God over Hell, and then I would also have God to blame should my husband not want to take me back. I was thinking I could even use God as a convincing factor if my husband was wavering in his decision. "God says we have to be together or we'll burn in Hell." I contemplated its use as a defense mechanism, too. "I don't WANT to be with you...but God's

MAKING me." I had so many emotions tumbling wildly through my mind that night it made me almost dizzy. Of them, the most disturbing thing I experienced was a fear of rejection. First, it started as a fear that my husband and children would reject me and tell me they were happier without me. Then, there were fears that my extended family would reject me because they disagreed with my husband's decision to take me back.

Finally, the most unbearable fear came when *God didn't come.* At least, He didn't show up the way I expected Him to. After all that time begging Him to supernaturally enter my bedroom and blackmail me with curses from Hell, He decided NOT to. Instead, He began to minister directly to my heart in LOVE. Love was like a dirty word to me at the time and I really wanted nothing to do with it. I was more interested in hanging out with anger, resentment and bitterness it seemed. Turns out, God knows how to speak my kind of love language. There were no threats. There were no curses. There were no visions of fiery damnation. There weren't even raised voices, hot tempers, or dirty looks. Looking back, I don't even think God spoke to me any kind of word that I could relay to you right now. My heart was simply changed and I was suddenly convinced.

I began to weep right there in my bedroom, and it didn't take very long before I was giving my life to the Lord fully with reckless abandon. My heart was no longer my own and I was flooded with a deep, deep desire for my husband...for my family. I began begging God to show me how to love, and God answered that prayer very quickly. So quickly, in fact, that I grabbed my things and ran out the door! I rushed to my car at two o'clock in the morning and nervously fumbled with the keys. For just a second, I began to panic. *"What if I feel like this and it's a lie? What if he says 'no'? What if he's changed the locks or won't come to the door???"* I turned the key and started the car. Blaring in my ears through the speakers was a song by Wayne Watson cued perfectly to the lyric *"if she's given her first love away...then she can love you like nobody can, like nobody can."* Hidden in those lyrics was God's unspoken truth to my heart in the midst of my doubt. I no longer wondered if it was real. I really had just given my first love away to the Lord, and in turn He was going to show me how to love my husband and my family in a way I had never done before. Everything was really going to be all right.

I put the car in gear and began the longest five-mile drive of my life, crying and praying the entire way. Upon pulling into the drive at just after two in the morning, I noticed a shadow on the front step. There sat my husband. Even now I cry thinking back to this reunion. I got out of the car and without saying a word walked straight into his open arms. He whispered, "I've been waiting for you. I'm so glad you're home." We hugged there on the step in the middle of the wee morning hours for a very long time. And God, in His amazing grace and goodness to us, made our reunion one for the storybooks. Love made its home in our hearts that night and the only thing left to say was simply, "I love you."

Gathering our tears, the Lord gently moved us back into our home...only it was like no home we'd ever known. It was brand new. We stood in the kitchen, holding each other tightly, and we formally invited Jesus Christ to live with us forever and to make His home in our hearts, regardless of our address...which we didn't know at the time, was about to change.

"I waited patiently for the Lord; he turned to me and heard my cry. He lifted me out of the slimy pit, out of the mud and the mire; he set my feet on a rock and gave me a firm place to stand...may all who seek you rejoice and be glad in you; may those who long for your saving help always say, 'The LORD is great!'"

Psalm 40:1-2, 16

5

Twin Towers

I kissed my husband good-bye for his first day of work in our new town. It was beautiful and I was just getting used to the time change in our new home state of Kansas. Having moved there only a few days prior to live with my husband's family, a Godly family that offered a significant support system to our new-found faith, I was still getting acclimated to my surroundings. I decided to turn on the local newscast in hopes of getting a better feel for the area. I watched (gripped in fear), the unfolding of the day we all know now as "9/11." This is the point where countless sad stories could be told. Almost everyone has one or more from that day.

For my purposes in this journey, though, I'm choosing not to tell them. Not that they aren't worth telling. All of them are tragedies that will mark and scar human history forever. In the years following this tragedy, however, there have been a remarkable number of testimonies rising from the rubble. As I reflect on this time, the Lord reminds me of my own.

As this horrid reality unfolded, I sat in the upstairs loft of my in-law's home, ALONE. Now, I had only been walking with the Lord for several weeks, and I had only been living in the state of Kansas for a few days. And here I was now face to face with a horrific human tragedy unfolding before my eyes. We all were. In that moment, however, as the Twin Towers would fall...I would have my own strong towers rise up within me. God had NO reason why He should comfort me. I was miles and miles away from the danger. God had NO reason to make sure my fear didn't overcome me. There were much greater needs at the time. Yet, not only did God do those very things, but He also constructed within me two other very significant things that I have been extremely grateful for. One was a tower of compassion. It sounds strange, but I hadn't had opportunity to experience true compassion before that day. It was life-changing for me. I sat silent and heard the Lord ask me, according to Romans 12:15 to, **"rejoice with those who rejoice and mourn with those who mourn."** As I was overcome with the Lord's compassion for His people, He then called me to intercede for them. This was the second tower God

47

strengthened within me that day. I didn't even know what intercession was, but God gave me a grand tour of these new structures erected within me. He began to teach me how to pray. He invited me to learn how to truly share in another's burden.

He began to erect these two vital things: compassion and intercession, inside my heart that day; and they have not been easily torn down. No matter the storm I'm weathering...no matter the war I'm waging, I can always look inside and find them standing erect and true. They serve as both a reminder of the Lord's compassion and unfailing love, and also as a calling to intercede on behalf of those who may need their very own strong tower, in a time of "sinking sand" all around them.

"From the ends of the earth I call to you, I call as my heart grows faint; lead me to the rock that is higher than I. For you have been my refuge, a strong tower against the foe."

Psalm 61:2-3

I am approaching the 10th Anniversary marker in my walk with the Lord; and during these years of strolling alongside Him, the Lord has provided many different opportunities for me to exercise my prayer-life and develop intercession "skills" that seem more purposeful, steady, and comfortable as I gain valuable experience and instruction from Him.

When the Lord first erected these towers of compassion and intercession within me, I had trouble controlling the compassion part; and feelings of deep compassion were usually accompanied by bouts of intense weeping. I remember the Lord calling me to intercede for Israel one day in particular. I was overwhelmed by a deep sorrow and compassion that far outweighed any prayer "work" I thought I was accomplishing. But because of the temporary discomfort I was experiencing during the uncontrollable bouts of weeping, I found myself suddenly reluctant to approach the Lord with a prayerful heart.

God began to instruct me regarding the tears I often shed during times of intercession. Lamentations 3:48-51 says, *"Streams of tears flow from my eyes because my people are destroyed. My eyes will flow unceasingly, without relief, until the LORD looks down from heaven and sees. What I see brings grief to my soul..."*

Finally, I began to have some understanding that weeping was a natural reaction that could be expected when a person felt the urgency of a burden revealed by God.

Waltzing with the Lord in prayer, as if dancing to an "Intercession Interlude," has been both work and pleasure. But, I remember a season where it seemed like MORE WORK than pleasure. One day that sticks out in my mind happened to be a Sunday during our church service. The presence of the Lord was ministering (to nearly all of the members of the congregation) in love; romancing and wooing the hearts of men and women in ways they had never experienced with God before. It was as if the Lord was sweeping everyone off their feet...everyone, that is, except ME.

The Lord called me into a place of deep intercession that day. He took me into a more mature place of prayer than I had ever been before. What was different about this experience was that this place of intercession was extremely laborious. It really felt like WORK. That may seem strange to relate it to you as work, but I felt as though I was emotionally, spiritually and even physically working harder than I had ever worked before. The perplexing facet of this story is the fact that I didn't understand a single second of what was happening, really. I was praying in "tongues" (see 1 Corinthians 12) for the duration of the service.

After church that day, I had some errands to run in town. During that time, I reflected on what had happened at church earlier that day. Truth be told, I was a little bit angry. I guess you might call me jealous, actually. I wanted to be wooed by the Lord; romanced and danced about as I had witnessed most of the members of my church family experiencing that very morning!

Frustrated, I prayed, confessing my feelings of jealousy and hurt; inquiring as to when it would be MY turn to experience Him as *lover of my soul*. Feeling like an abused secretary, I felt the Lord speak to my heart saying, *"Sometimes, I just need you to do my bidding. I'll let you know when it's time for something else."* That just frustrated me further! Sinking into a jealous rage, I threw a temper tantrum. Again, I plead my case with the Lord, inquiring of Him as to when I would be the "secretary that gets to have an affair with her Boss?!?" (In hindsight, I don't think I should have approached the Lord using metaphorical infidelity as my rebuttal argument.) I'm embarrassed to admit that I even shook my fist at the Lord telling Him that I wasn't sure if I was even IN LOVE with Him. I just hadn't ever experienced the romantic feelings that a person typically has when they are falling IN LOVE. Of course, He had no interest in indulging my fit of rage and left me to myself the rest of the afternoon.

On the return drive home from doing errands in town, having felt the conviction of my sin, I repented and humbly came before Him; I surrendered to His calling on my life as an intercessor and my "job" as His "secretary." Just then, in the light of my contrition, I was flooded with a stomach full of butterflies and a face as flushed as it was the day I had my very first kiss!

Speaking to my spirit, the Lord said, "*See, I can give you butterflies and make you blush anytime I want to.*" In that instant, I absolutely fell head-over-heels in love with Him.

There could have been an extremely "sad story" written into the pages of my life had I not embraced the Lord's calling on me as an intercessor. I'm thankful that over the last 10 years He has gradually and patiently instructed me, training me "*on the job*" (so to speak); and I'm grateful that He has been allowing me to mature and develop in ways that have helped me become an asset to my "employer."

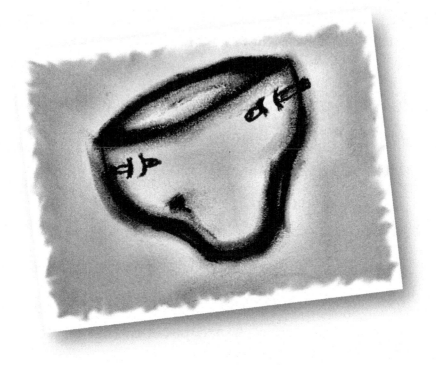

6

It's a Boy

Congratulations!

The events surrounding the birth of my third son, yes I said THIRD...were miraculous enough. I had God's hand all over me during that pregnancy and for that I was very grateful. Things could have gone tragically wrong because we lived over an hour from the hospital, and there were unsuspected complications. It was discovered that my 8.5 lb baby boy had turned to breech position, requiring a C-section for delivery. It was only AFTER the C-section had begun that the doctor discovered an undetected placenta previa as well.

All this was clearly organized by the Lord as He graciously held my life and the life of my new baby boy in His hands. Thank You, Lord! Had he not caused the 8+ lb baby to somehow flip completely over inside my belly without me noticing it, and had He not caused the doctor to "have a feeling" she should perform a last minute sonogram, we would have never gone in for the emergency C-section, which at the time wasn't exactly an emergency. But because of the distance I lived from the hospital, the baby presenting feet-first, and my full term status, there was no way the doctor was sending me home without delivering me safely. Only after the section had begun did they realize the true emergency...my placenta had begun rupturing! In other words, my placenta had begun tearing away from the wall of my uterus, so that the baby could have lost his blood supply. That could have been life-threatening for me or my baby! Again, testimony time...thank You, Lord! However, the real testimony that I can't help but share is one of the "tearing" of my heart...

It's challenging to discuss this one without touching base on a little of the sad story, but I'll do my best. I'll just keep it simple by telling you that as a woman who did NOT have a good mother-daughter relationship in her life, I was DESPERATE to have a daughter of my own, in hopes of establishing one. I had my first son shortly after one of the most significant sad stories in my life. The second son came after another significant sad story.

I began seeing a theme there and refused to have another child because I just knew it meant something bad would happen again and/or then I'd have another boy. (This part of my life was lived out before my husband and I began walking with the Lord.) Now that we had this new love and this life of hope, we found ourselves excited for the birth of this third child. I would be lying if I said I didn't struggle at first. I was scared that I wouldn't love this baby if it were a third boy. I may have even prayed for a girl specifically. That makes me cringe to say that, but I may have!

I fight back tears even now as I think back to greeting this third boy of mine on his birthday. As I have already told you, the birth in and of itself was a miracle! The fact that I loved him with a jealous love before I even met him is a testimony! However, there was a different kind of testimony also taking place during the birth of my third son. It actually DOES go back to that yearning for a mother-daughter relationship I'd never had. It wasn't until after all the hustle and bustle of having a newborn subsided that God began to reveal to me what had occurred.

One day, as I *oogled* at the perfect baby boy in my arms, I asked God if He understood my heart in asking Him for a mother-daughter relationship. I tried explaining it to Him, but really it was just an unspoken void that I wanted the Lord to fill. However, I didn't want Him to ever think that I was ungrateful for this beautiful bundle of boy in my arms. This God of ours knows us so well! He explained to ME what I was feeling, and then gave me a glimpse of the work He'd started. In that moment my heart began to receive understanding.

Up to now, I've not mentioned her, but this testimony has a name. Formally, she is Mother-in-Law. I've come to think of her only as Mom. God has such a way of doing things! He showed me that before I could BE the kind of mother I always wanted to be to my OWN daughter, I needed to experience being the daughter in a healthy mother-daughter relationship rooted in God's Love.

That day, I thought of everything my Mother-in-Law and I had ever talked about, prayed about, laughed about or cried about. I thought about her face and her hands. I thought about the way she loves the Lord and the fact that I could see in her eyes that she loved me, and not out of obligation but by choice. I thought about Delivery Day in the operating room as I lay on the table about to have my C-section, and how SHE was by my side, meeting my third son for the first time. I'd never had a mother at the previous two births. God knew before I did how important it was for my ears to hear "I love you, Daughter." He'd begun the process of establishing a mother-daughter relationship that

I could not be more grateful for...one that makes it easy to say, "I love you, too, Mom."

7

Dreams, Visions and

Revisions

"In the last days, God says,
I will pour out my spirit on all people.
Your sons and daughters will prophesy,
Your young men will see visions,
Your old men will dream dreams."
--Acts 2:17

From the very beginning of my walk with the Lord, I began experiencing dreams and visions. My church family and my in-laws were always encouraging me to write them down and often times they would meet with me to pray over them and seek the Lord for an interpretation. I was never very good at interpreting them...but I was always astounded by what the Lord would reveal by His Spirit.

I smile, even now, thinking back to these times. He seemed to pour out lavishly. I think the enemy did, too, as I began to experience frightening nightmares as well. In keeping with the theme of this book, I will forego the telling of the sad stories. I don't know that there is a direct testimony coming out of the fact that I experienced dreams and visions, except maybe the fact that God is faithful to His Word as seen in Acts 2:17:

> "In the last days, God says,
> I will pour out my spirit on all people.
> Your sons and daughters will prophesy,
> Your young men will see visions,
> Your old men will dream dreams."

Also, the fact that my church body at the time was absolutely convinced that it was actually God speaking through me. I was the "new girl!" I was young, immature and frightened a lot of the time! I didn't know any scripture from memory and I still struggled with worldly sins. I had a potty-mouth that wasn't so easily cast off as it was for my husband. I found that during stressful times, I would light up a cigarette instead of allowing the light of the Lord to shine into those places of my life. Even so, I was trying to bring those areas, albeit slowly, under the submission, authority and direction of the Lord. My church family was so supportive! I became very comfortable sharing my dreams and/or visions with them. It wasn't a threatening task at all. As I reflect on this even now, I feel the Lord is showing me that this was the beginning of His working through my *fear of man.* In this area, I am still a "work in progress." Let me leap forward at this point to share the memory that is dropping into my mind this very moment.

One Saturday, a special church service was being held up in one of the very large cities about an hour away from our hometown. My congregation was organizing a caravan to attend and my husband and I decided to go. This service was one centered around "Miracles and Healings." I never had much faith in the area of healings. I still struggle. Let me clarify this for a moment – I believe with my entire being that God is fully CAPABLE TO HEAL – but I find that I am always ready to believe that He is rarely WILLING TO HEAL. With that in mind, I was excited and nervous to attend this service. I was skeptical, too, that the things I would witness from sitting in my seat might just be a hoax. After all, I didn't know these people! I didn't trust them!

As my mind continued to work overtime during the long commute, I became suddenly overwhelmed by an intense fear of man. I just KNEW they were going to pick on me! I had this feeling that somehow, the pastor was going to point at me, call me out and lay bare all of my *junk* right there in front of everyone. The fact that I still felt so far-off from achieving the status of "good Christian" was only the tip of the iceberg concerning my fears. I am also a very tall woman. I am also an overweight woman. Insecurities the size of CONTINENTS! Those are some of the sad stories to which I refer. Without delving into all of that, I will just tell you, that at this point I had determined to remain as INvisible as possible during this entire service.

I stood in the row with my church group mouthing words to songs I didn't necessarily know. I worshiped with one eye open to make sure I didn't get too "outside of the box" and unintentionally draw attention to myself. I had this internal dialogue with myself (and probably with the Lord) about how silly I was being. Part of me wanted to just LET GO and experience God in this new freedom that everyone else had apparently found. The other part of me was terrified. I remember that as we sang the praise and worship songs the muscles in my arms began to burn because my arms wanted to do their own thing! They wanted to go straight up into the air and worship! I wanted them to stay stiff at my sides...this battle between me and my own arms makes me laugh! It's the truth, though. Here's when it happened. Just as I suspected, the pastor raised his arm, pointed his finger and described what I was wearing directly into the microphone. WHAT?!? Yes, he did. Calling me forward, he begins to tell the audience that God had revealed to him that I had an intense *fear of man* issue that the Lord wanted to deliver me from. By this time, I was wearing my ugly cry. You know the face. The cry that you don't want anyone to see...and I was wearing it in front of all these people! At this point it didn't matter, as there was no turning back. I decided that if God was going to go to all this trouble just to help me find a freedom to worship Him with reckless abandon, then just maybe He didn't necessarily mind the chubby arms I lifted in praise. Just maybe the off-pitch key of my voice, fumbling its way through songs I didn't know wasn't as big a deal as I thought.

With one look into my eyes, the pastor knew he'd touched on the matter of my heart. Then placing his hand on my forehead I went down and out for the count. I don't really remember what happened as I lay on the floor in front of hundreds of people. I could easily panic even today wondering if my shirt had come up too far to expose my jelly-roll. Instead, I prefer to think about what happened next. All I remember is walking back to my seat and worshiping my God with a freedom I'd never known...and for the duration of the service I COULD NOT put my arms down! God held them up the entire time and I didn't care who was watching. I believe God had begun a process of delivering me from the fear of man that night. I can now worship freely (most of the time).

Realizing at this point that I have gone off topic for a moment, I am drawn back to the sticky note in hand. As I read the verse from Acts 2:17 and remember the times God lavishly poured out dreams and visions even on me, I think I was being prepared for times when God would need to move supernaturally in and around my life. I wasn't suddenly startled by the events I witnessed at this church service in which the bondage-breaking power of the Lord fell upon me and began severing the stronghold that the fear of man had on me. I had seen the Lord time and again, in my dreams and visions, do things such as this.   Even now, as I think back upon those feelings I was churning over in my mind during the long caravan ride up to the service, it was as if I KNEW ahead of time that this sort of thing might happen.   Was it an expectation even? I am not sure what it was, but I know one thing for sure.   Had I not experienced the Lord in so many supernatural ways within my dreams and visions, and seen for myself how He moved...I WOULDN'T HAVE MOVED when He prompted me that night.

Once again, His ways and timing were perfectly crafted for my good. *"For I know the plans I have for you,'" declares the Lord, "plans to prosper you and not to harm you, plans to give you a hope and a future." Jeremiah 29:11.*

__Snapshots of Me__

By Amber Dobson Woodrum

I look around and all I see;
Are people looking back at me.

Sometimes I feel like a snapshot to the world;
In living color; but captured, still...

I do have dreams locked inside;
Are these peering eyes what cause my dreams to
hide?

I have such fear of what these eyes think of me;
Overcoming these fears would
set my dreams free!

Oh, Lord, let this one thing be true...
In their snapshots of me,

LET THEM SEE PICTURES OF YOU.

While addressing this issue of the *fear of man,* I wanted to share with you the fact that I still struggle often with it. It's an easy thing for Satan to target; especially in lives of women, it seems. We live in a culture that has a very narrow view of what is considered acceptable...let alone beautiful. And don't think for a second that it's just us chubbier gals that struggle with the *fear of man.* Some of the most desperate, severe struggles with the *fear of man* caused by low self-esteem and self-hatred were seen in the lives of MEN I know. In the light of this all-too-common problem, are there ways to *conquer* instead of only *cope?*

Fortunately, we don't have to look very far to find help. God's Word helps me look at myself with a fresh perspective when it seems that I can't see past my own reflection; a reflection that is often distorted by past experiences, present anguish or even future fears.

The world loves to tell us who we are and where we belong; and it's often a major contradiction to who the Word of God says we are. Maybe you still struggle with the *fear of man*, and you often find yourself paralyzed.

Can you identify times in your life when the *fear of man* has kept you from moving out of your comfort-zone in obedience to DO or SAY something the Holy Spirit was prompting? I would encourage you to go to God's Word and seek out scriptures that can help you see yourself in the same light that He does.

~~~~~~~

"...show me your face, let me hear your voice; for your voice is sweet, and your face is lovely."

Song of Songs 2:14

~~~~~~

BEAUTIFUL ENCOUNTER

I say, "Beautiful Encounter..."
At this world You've made.
"Beautiful Encounter..."
At the grass fields' every blade.

I say, "Beautiful Encounter..."
At every color on every rose.
"Beautiful Encounter..."
At every sunset sky and the majesty it
shows.

I say, "Beautiful Encounter..."
At every moonlit night.
"Beautiful Encounter..."
At the dawn's new light.

I say, "Beautiful Encounter..."
At every wave on every sea.
You say, "Beautiful Encounter..."
At every glimpse of me.

> *"Fear of man will prove to be a snare, but whoever trusts in the LORD is kept safe."*
> -   Proverbs 29:25

> *"For God wanted them to know that the riches and glory of Christ are for you...too. And this is the secret: Christ lives in you. This gives you assurance of sharing his glory."*
> -   *Colossians 1:27 NLT*

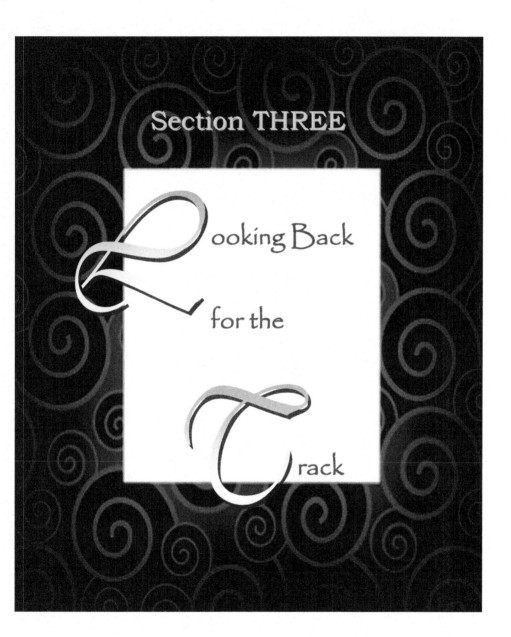

Section THREE

$\mathcal{L}$ooking Back

for the

$\mathcal{T}$rack

8

Back to My Roots

As I was planning to prepare the next chapter of this book, I found myself sitting in the pew at church with my mouth hanging open and tears falling from my eyes. My husband, who was sitting next to me, leaned over and whispered, "This ain't no quinky-dink." I agreed that this was no *coincidence*. The Sunday message, as delivered by many members of our church body, quickly spoke to our hearts. From the feeling in the room, to the Pastor's word, to a poem one sweet lady felt led to share, to the final thought given by the pastor's son...all of it confirmed to our hearts exactly what God was doing with the process He had me going through in the writing of this book. While we are friends with the families, they did NOT know the happenings of the last week...how I had finally become stuck in the mud with no clear direction from the Lord. They knew nothing of my resolve to turn around and take my walk back, and then proceed again down the path once traveled with my loving Lord.

There's no way they could have known how I planned to find strength in the testimonies and remembrances of my journey with the Lord Jesus...strength that would give me the ability to persevere through the current storms I need to weather. I was overwhelmed as the pastor's son walked to the microphone and said, "*I just want to encourage you, that if you find you are at a place in your life that feels like there is no clear leading from the Lord, then go back to your roots. Go with Him again to those places in your life where you could see Him working and leading you. Draw from those testimonies."*

Very interesting. That's what I had decided to do only days earlier. That decision is exactly why I am writing this book! Looks like the Lord knew exactly how to confirm to my husband and myself that we are on the right track...the right foot...no, no...the *right page.*

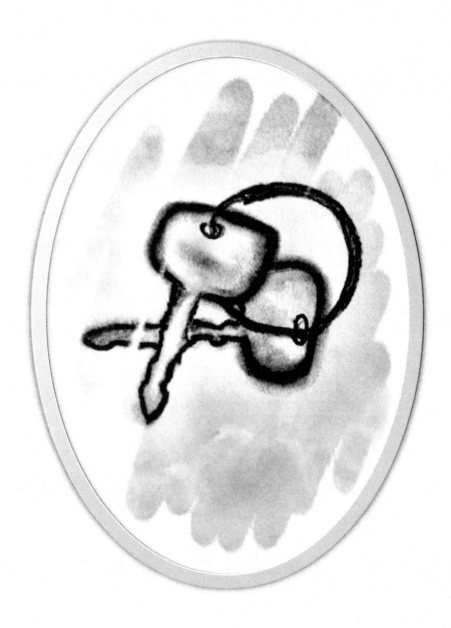

9

Bessie

Gentle
Green
Giant

I chuckle as I begin to write this chapter. Have you ever wondered *"What's in a name?"* As I use an Internet search engine to look up the meaning to the name of this chapter's title, I find myself enthused by the result. According to the results of many of the most popular name origin sites, Bessie is most commonly used in

English and is interpreted as "God is my Oath." Of course, I didn't have any idea of this meaning when I bestowed that name upon my car. Yes, you heard right. I named my car. Bessie is the perfect name for her and you would undoubtedly agree if you were to meet her. She is a big, green mini-van. She has been a very good "friend" to me for the last six years. My family has made countless memories within the confines of her interior. However, she has...as of late...become bitter in her old age. She's almost unbearable to be around. Matter of fact, she makes up quite a few sad stories of mine all on her own. Continuing the theme, again, means that we are NOT going to revisit those less-than-fond thoughts in lieu of sharing the happier times, when Bessie was a beautiful part of my life. I still drive around in Bessie to this day, but my "attitude of gratitude" while behind her wheel has been less than enthusiastic recently. It's time to make a U-turn and head back down the road until we find a better disposition.

The first pit-stop we'll make is the day I dreamed of her. I was driving a rather fantastic Jeep at the time, but it had way too many miles on it and there was no way our growing family could fit into it anymore. My oldest son, bless his heart, had lines dug into his hips from squeezing himself into the middle between two infant car seats! Time to get a new car. It was going to be a mini-van which best suited our needs at the time. I began looking at cars online and found this particular style and color that I just loved immediately. I don't know why, but I get pretty excited over a change in cars. I have never in my lifetime had a brand new car, and I don't really ever expect to. For some reason, however, I thoroughly enjoy getting a new, USED vehicle.

This one I found online was many states away and not a possibility at all. Nevertheless, I dreamt every night about this metallic green van with tinted windows and a sleek little design. The problem was that no matter how far up and down the interstate I searched, I couldn't find one even remotely like it! It was the strangest thing. I began to get discouraged.

Then, one day I was working in the front office of a real estate company, and it was a very slow afternoon. All of the agents were out. The broker was out. The phone was dead. So I spent some time thinking about this van and praying about the Lord's provision for the van. I felt the Lord whisper to my spirit, *"Ask Me for it. Ask Me for what you dream of."* Did I dare ask for this specific van? Did I dare ask the Lord for a specific color?!? I felt as if I was on a hidden camera show, and at any minute I would be made a laughing stock for even considering that what I heard was the Lord actually inviting me to ask Him, specifically, for what I wanted. As a way of being discreet from potential on-lookers, I whispered to myself the prayer with all the specifics I had, and then began to search for a picture on the Internet of the exact vehicle I dreamed of. I wanted one that I could print out.

Finally I found it, printed it in full color, and held onto it. I was determined to believe God had spoken to me that day. I took the picture home and showed my husband, telling him a vivid account of how God had spoken to me about it. I even admitted that I believed He would give it to me. My husband looked at me with the wonder of a child shining brightly through his baby-blue eyes, and in faith, exclaimed "Amen!"

I am not exaggerating when I share with you what happened on the VERY NEXT DAY. I had to run to a small town 20 miles from home for groceries, when I passed a small "mom and pop" car dealership. There on the lot, sat the exact vehicle I had been wanting!!! Color, body, make, model, year...EVERYTHING I ASKED FOR! I drove my Bessie home that night.

God is so amazing to me when I relive this testimony in my mind. You could say I've recently been kind of in the muck regarding my car. (Again, it's a sad story and I am not going to tell it.) However, I choose to remind myself that six years and many thousands of miles ago, Bessie was hand-picked for me by my loving God. He gave me my dream car that day! That blows my mind. Now while things aren't so smooth with Bessie as of late, and I have different needs and dreams as far as our next family vehicle is concerned, I can honestly say that this gift from the Lord has been HUGE, and I had let myself forget it...until now.

Even as I think back on our six years with Bessie, I can only think of ONE time that she had to have any kind of significant repair work, and that was for the air conditioning. She wasn't cooling anymore, and we lived in Kansas where it gets mighty hot. We just dealt with it until I became pregnant with a mid-July due date. You can bet we found the money somewhere for that repair! Other than that, we've had nothing in six years. Only now has anything begun to shut down, and I think that is an incredible record! Thank You, Lord! You are so good to us!

At this point, the pit-stops we have made down this road may not be sequential or even make a lot of sense in your mind. However, these are snippets of wonderful things that happened or moments that I consider remarkable enough to mention. All of them, mind you, are purposeful to bring me back to a place of joy, gratitude, trust, faith, hope and perseverance to get through some of the sad stories that have tried to keep me here in the muck.

I have always under-rated the importance of a rearview mirror. I can say that now because I haven't had one for the last several years. That could easily tempt me into telling a sad story, but we'll just veer around that pothole. Of course rearview mirrors are great for giving us a better visual of the road, and for keeping us from backing into things outside our vehicle. One day, though, it gave me a wonderful glimpse of something going on INSIDE my vehicle.

Normally, my children are not very quiet while I'm driving. They have their own little conversations that can even provide pretty good entertainment to the passengers up front. This day though, as I was driving, I realized that my surroundings were just about silent. I hadn't noticed immediately. I was busy praying to the

Lord about the previous nights' worship service at our church. There had been a special evening service that was almost entirely worship. I loved those nights. My husband and I went with the kids to the service in hopes of getting fully immersed in the flow of the Spirit pouring out from the worship time. I was disappointed that the children weren't behaving very well, and we had to leave early. I missed out on something that I really felt I needed. Again, I had begun to discuss this with the Lord as I drove, when I suddenly noticed the silence in my car. I looked in the rearview mirror to be certain I hadn't forgotten my children, or maybe to check that they were all okay. What I saw in my rearview mirror took my breath away and I just began to weep. (I remember giving this testimony a week later during our regular church service and even then I was choked up.) There sat all four of my children safely buckled into their car seats.

Baby girl was sleeping and her three older brothers had their hands raised in worship to the Lord. Suddenly I realized that I could hear the faint playing of a familiar song on the radio. I turned it up a bit and watched my three sons worship the Lord to the song "Our God is an Awesome God" through my rearview mirror. That moment far exceeded every single expectation my heart had for the part of the worship service I missed out on the preceding night, and the presence of the Lord fell upon us right there inside ol' Bessie. (Actually, I think it was one of her happiest days!) Our God IS an awesome God!!!!

Another thought about Bessie just makes me chuckle!

I love remembering how God has loved to use Bessie as a piggy bank in the last six years. Many, many times, I can recall finding wads of money (just when I needed them most) stuffed in the glove box, the ashtray, the center console, sitting on the driver's seat or even under the floor mat. Still to this day, I don't know a single person responsible for those monies...but God!

My family has been fortunate enough to take many road trips over the years. It is easily our favorite past-time and our favorite way of vacationing. We've driven Bessie from Kansas to Michigan and back again more times than I can count! We've driven her down to the Missouri Ozarks. We've driven her on a 10-day caravan from Kansas to Washington State, stopping at several major parks and/or camping spots along the way. We've driven on west coast beaches and we've driven her to volcano viewing points! We've driven Bessie across the border and half-way through Canada. We've driven her to more baseball games than I can count. We've parked her in every type of garage. We've eaten every type of food inside of her and have enjoyed picnics with her. We've been transported home from the hospital after the birth of two of my children, and we've transported these four children back to the hospital at one time or another. We've gotten sick in her. We've changed diapers in her. We've loaned her out and gotten her back many times. We've enjoyed drive-in movies with her and she's faithfully participated in countless successful grocery-getting trips. So many memories!

The one that really sticks out the most to me right now is the time we drove to Branson, Missouri as a family. I was 8 ½ months pregnant with my last child and it was over 100 degrees during this weeklong vacation! I was an emotional yo-yo. One minute we were loving the pool and the condo we stayed at. Or then just a little later, we were laughing hysterically at the race track as I watched my husband overcome his extreme dizziness in order to drive the same track multiple times so each boy would have equal lap counts. They were too small to drive themselves, so he'd selflessly driven each one on his lap...round and round.

The next minute it seemed we were screaming at strangers or at each other while stuck in the worst traffic jams I had ever experienced up to that point. I have never met such crazy drivers as the ones I encountered in Branson. I didn't want to holler at the kids...they weren't the ones driving. I didn't even really want to holler at my husband. It was everyone else sending me into a hormonal surge that felt like electrical currents of fury racing through me.

Finally, one exhaustively HOT afternoon, we got stuck in terrible, terrible traffic on what I would call a near 90-degree angle hill. Okay, so I'm not accurate with that probably, but you get the idea. There we were in Bessie, stuck in this position that felt like the super-slow climb of a roller coaster making its way to the top of the first hill. We'd try to inch forward only to roll backward. We'd nearly slam the people in front, and then those in the rear of us! We went back and forth like this for more than 20 minutes! The blood was rushing to my head. I was hot. I was very, very pregnant and I could feel the supercharged fury beginning to rev up. Finally, we had nearly made our way to the top of the hill where there was a four-way traffic light. There were three cars in front of us when the light turned green...but Bessie wasn't moving. She began to roll backwards, and in that amount of time the traffic light turned back to yellow very quickly! All at once the supercharged fury inside of me came out and the passer-by's on the street stopped and stared. My husband KNEW he'd better not miss that light! He floored the gas pedal, and poor Bessie, our Gentle Green Giant BURNED RUBBER in downtown Branson,

Missouri!!!! Squealing her tires and leaving the horrid smell of a dirty race track behind, we almost lost control and barely made it through the stop light. I was so absolutely mortified that my husband had PEELED OUT in a 1998 Pontiac Mini-Van that I thought I would go into labor right then and there! Of course, I laugh thinking about this now...but it seemed so dramatic at the time. Now several years later it's one of my favorite memories of our times in ol' Bessie, and if burnin' rubber on the mini-van is all that my husband and I have had to scream about after all these years with Bessie, then I'd say she's been a keeper.

Over the course of six years, I'm sure I could write an entire book around only the adventures we've had with Bessie. For my purpose here, though, I wanted to regain a sense of thankfulness for her...gratefulness for the Lord's provision of her, and a hope that God will again meet our need for a new car as He sees fit. He just did it so well the first time that I'd really like to trust Him with it again. Now THAT feels like I'm on the right track!

10

Thinking Out Loud

"A Mom's expression (in response) to God; reflecting on the way God's Word affects her daily life."

Looking back to the earlier years in my walk with the Lord brings me to a season in my life that I have come to know as *Thinking Out Loud.*

I have always wanted to be a writer. Even as a little girl and onward into high school, I thrived in my English classes. I especially loved the poetry semesters! I truly believed that *Thinking*

Out Loud would be the title to my first collection of poems. There was a season in my life where it seemed that no matter the emotion I was having that day, it would spring forth a short collection of whimsically rhyming words. I really thought the Lord was going to finally make my dream come true. Writing would become a full-scale profession! I was going to be famous and make enough money to no longer be JUST a stay-at-home mom. Oh, to be young again! Frankly, I was living in La-La Land! For starters, being a stay-at-home mom should never be paired with the word JUST in a sentence. Enough said there. Secondly, my aspirations for being a writer, becoming famous and making the big money from a New York Times bestseller were not glorifying to the Lord. It grieves my spirit even now, looking back and seeing the greed that once was laced throughout my desire to write. I pray and hope that all these years later, my heart motives have changed...and I believe that they have.

But during this especially poetic season of my life, the Lord would pour out these cute little poems that impacted me greatly. I would write them down and sometimes even share them with people as deemed appropriate. I was so in love with the Lord for allowing me to write things that I felt were absolutely inspired by Him. Unfortunately, as much as I am ashamed to admit it...there's a sad story here, too. It involved the motive of my heart at that time, and the only part of it that I will share with you is that this sad story has lasted for six years.

Remembering that we aren't sharing our sad stories, it's with a happier tone that I look back at some of the poems I've saved over these last six years. These were times that God was speaking to me directly in a language that I longed to hear. Tears swell in my eyes even now as I remember the romance of it. I would never have called it that before...a *romance*. That's what it was, though. I've almost forgotten what it meant to me to have the Lord speak to me that way. It created such an expectation in me...such anticipation in my heart! It's more than enough that God was just speaking, let alone speaking to me in the love language of my heart...romancing me through that season of my life.

As I sit here, I have the old binder of poems on my lap. Because of the sad story I'm not telling, I haven't saved that many of them. However, there are a few that were extra special to me. Some of them were the Lord's way of humoring me through a situation. I think the Lord has a great sense of humor!

(This poem was written for my oldest two boys who were fighting because their little brother was annoying them by playing copy cat.)

COPY CAT

Copy Cat, Copy Cat
Tit for Tat

Today I learned that my Copy Cat
Really isn't all that bad

What made me think twice said,
"Imitate Me as I imitate Christ"

So, when you copy ME,
You really copy HIM...

What about that can be so grim?

Now, Copy Cat, Copy Cat
Tit for Tat

Go ahead and copy me
I'm alright with that.

Other poems were inspired directly by the Word of God. It's one of the ways the Lord would translate a scripture in a way that made it applicable to me in that moment. He would make sense of it for me through a poem.

Let's look at a short example:

> *Hebrews 6:9 – "...we are confident of better things in your case – things that accompany salvation."*

<u>Hebrews 6:9</u>

Let there be in my reflection;
The things that accompany salvation

The things that accompany salvation
In me.

I've known You as my Savior
But I know that there's more...
I've known You as my Savior;
Reveal yourself...as LORD.

I'm not sure what to call the poems He inspired me to write for other people, but often I received a poem for a friend or a family member out of my prayer time for them. I remember Him giving me poetic stories and songs...often child-like ones that spoke directly to the parenting of my own children. I still sing one of the lullabies to my children today!

> *"We've got enough of Love's light,*
> *To brighten the sky at night...*
> *We've got enough Love songs,*
> *To make the whole world bright...*
> *We've got enough Love and*
> *understanding,*
> *For when times get tight...*
> *Because of God's LOVE,*
> *We're gonna be alright!"*

Just for fun, I'm going to include a few more of my poems here, along with how the Lord inspired them.

> *"...and to present her to Himself as a radiant church, without stain or wrinkle or any other blemish, but holy and blameless."*
>
> Ephesians 5:27

Shower Me

Looking for an outpouring,
Give me as much as you can.
Fill me up
With Your Holy Spirit;
Your presence is all I ask!

Shower me...make me clean.
Clean me...b'cause I want to be
Waterlogged...yet wrinkle free.
Shower me...Shower me.

Washed by your cleansing blood;
Cleansed with Your Holy hands...
Send Your spirit in like a flood;
Oh Lord! Saturate the land...
Saturate the land!

Shower me...make me clean.
Clean me...b'cause I want to be
Waterlogged...yet wrinkle free.
Shower me...Shower me.

<u>Shower Me</u> was actually a song that the Lord sang to me. It was life changing! I was running a daycare at the time and working very long hours. I tried to run a daycare that stayed open during the 2nd and 3rd shift jobs because there really wasn't childcare available during those hours in the area. Since it was run out of my home, it really wasn't too much of an inconvenience, and we needed the income. But my alone time with the Lord suffered. I had children around all the time! One day, I just about had enough of everything, and I longed to find my way into the undisturbed presence of the Lord.

That afternoon, when my husband got home from work, he suggested I take a break while he watched the children. I accepted and decided to use this rare opportunity to take a nice, long shower. As I stood under the water, I decided to multi-task and do some praying. I began with a lengthy prayer of repentance because I felt far-off from the Lord, exhausted physically and spiritually, and I was very sorry that the only time I could find to go to Him was during my shower. Even then I had to multi-task and couldn't focus on just Him! Oh, I was beating myself up! It was then that the Lord, in His graciousness, inspired the words to this song. It melted my heart because it was His way of telling me that He knew I was in a season of craziness. He graced us to get through it together. The fact that the song He released in me that day used the words "Shower Me" while I was actually coming to Him apologetically for being IN the shower...loosed a joy in my spirit like I'd never known! I laughed and cried simultaneously while singing this song in the shower. I think I stayed there long enough to use up all of the hot water that day.

~~~~~~

The next poem I'll share is one that came from the Lord to explain to me a scripture that was relevant for that day, in a way that I could really grasp and apply to my life. Simple...yet profound.

> *"...there are three things never satisfied, four that never say 'Enough'..."*
> Proverbs 17:15b

Lowly As I Am

Lowly as I am
You met with me again.

Even when I'm not satisfied
And never say "Enough."
Even when I fail to surrender
And give You all my love.
Even in my daily sins
Your mercies never end.

Lowly as I am
You met with me again.

~~~~~

This next poem is one that demonstrates how the Lord was speaking to me on behalf of someone else. While I was praying for a family that had recently suffered a tragedy, the Lord offered this poem and instructed my heart to write it in a card for them. I was obedient and did just that. I have never found out if they received it or if it meant anything to them...but even to this day it means a great deal to me.

> *"You are my hiding place; you will protect me from trouble and surround me with songs of deliverance."*
> Psalm 32:7

Pain and Promise

You look to the sky and wonder,
"How long will it rain?"
You're deaf from the thunder,
And drowning in its pain.

You question each cloud,
And long for blue skies…
Seems you'll never understand
Life's all-too-soon "Good-bye's."

But, the promise for you is:
The weather WILL change.
There's hope in that promise,
As you look toward better days.

So, even though it seems
You've stood in the cold too long;
And shivered through too many
Of the wind's sad songs…

There is One who has heard
your whisper of a cry;
He sings over you now
With His healing lullaby.

And though today it may seem
That you struggle to hear…
His Songs of Deliverance will one day be clear.

The last two poems I am going to share with you were ones the Lord brought out of me as a direct result of my emotions. The first was a prayerful response that I had during the very first day of my very first Women's Bible Study organized by my church.

My Prayer Poem

Loose me from my desires,
Entangle me in Yours.
Enter me into Your will,
Close every other door...

Open the eyes of my heart to see,
And use Your mighty hand;
To move me from my unbelief,
Into Your promised land.

~~~~~

Lastly, I'll share with you the second emotion-driven poem that the Lord drew out of the intense feelings I'd always wrestle with during times in which my father-in-law would travel overseas for missionary work. This particular trip was for a significant amount of time into a particularly dangerous country. Instead of wrestling with my overwhelming fears, however, the Lord gave me a glimpse of His overwhelming love for His people. My heart changed that day... and I responded with this poem, dedicated to my father-in-law, who shared with me that a copy of this poem is posted on a wall in his walk-in closet with some of his other "treasures."

<u>Now I Can See</u>

I've heard you talk of this love for years,
But I've never understood.
I could only see the danger;
The beauty and burden
I never could.

Eyes blinded through selfish tears,
Heart frozen from the fear;
I could never see a single face,
That would carry you to that far-off place.

But, as I've grown in the Lord,
And learned lessons in love;
I find my selfishness replaced
with burdens from above.

So, I ask your forgiveness for the years gone by,
For my selfishness to keep you home.
I see clearly now in my Father's eye...
And have fallen in love with a people
I've never known.

Six years ago, I closed my book of poetry to open it only twice since. The first time I revisited this time of my life and the poems in my book, it was painful for me to discover that I had exalted the "sad story" found within it's pages higher than the Author Himself. Today, however as I open it again, the Author of my heart and the Finisher of my faith has found a way to inspire me once again...and there's something beautifully poetic about that.

"...let us run with endurance the race that is set

before us, looking unto Jesus, the author and finisher

of our faith..."

Hebrews 12:1-2 NKJV

Section FOUR

Finding Hidden Treasure

"Teach me to do your will, for you are my God. May your gracious Spirit lead me forward on a firm footing."

Psalm 143:10

11

Finding the Hidden

Treasures

"I want them to be encouraged and knit together by strong ties of love. I want them to have complete confidence that they understand God's mysterious plan, which is Christ himself. In him lie hidden all the treasures of wisdom and knowledge. I am telling you this so no one will deceive you with well-crafted arguments. For though I am far away from you, my heart is with you. And I rejoice that you are living as you should and that your faith in Christ is strong."

Colossians 2:2-5 NLT

The sad story that marks this chapter is heavily outweighed by the testimony of God's provision, grace, love, mercy, patience, kindness...I could go on forever.

The above scripture is the one that the Lord has imprinted on my heart in regards to the adventure of our life known as HOME-SCHOOL.

The Lord gently nudged my heart for a number of years regarding homeschooling. He even gave me close friends who were homeschooling their own families – a valuable resource to have at your fingertips! The sad stories that have been paved over on this part of my journey were made up primarily of one hefty helping of stubbornness, a handful of fear, a dash of uncertainty and just a small pinch of faith...stirred all together in a big bowl of disobedience! Take my word for it – you don't need a taste of that. Yuck!

Instead, I want to tell you about the day that I fell to my knees in the middle of my bedroom and surrendered to the will of the Lord. I can see myself there even now...on my knees with my arms stretched upward in the shape of a V. I tilted my head back, lifted my eyes beyond myself, beyond the walls of my room, and looked straight into my Father's eyes. It's the first time I'd ever screamed out loud to the Lord. "FINE, GOD! HAVE IT YOUR WAY!" That's all I had to say and the Lord knew He had my fully surrendered heart. The reason I was on my knees in the first place was a big part of that bad (and sad) recipe I spoke of earlier. Leaves a bad taste in my mouth even now! When people ask me how I came to the decision to home-school, I have to tell them the Lord called me to do it. He did. When they ask me how He called me, I find it hard to articulate. He called me gently at first...but by the end, there was an event with my children and the public school which they attended that proved to be "the straw that broke the camel's back." Let me just say at this point, that I am actually quite fond of the local school system and have no opinions either way regarding public school in general. My daughter attends the public preschool and all of my boys play sports for that school district. I don't think for a second that God was revealing to me any problem within that particular school or making a statement about public school overall. I believe He had to allow this particular incident to occur in a way that would facilitate my full surrender to Him. I went kicking and eventually screaming, but once He had my full surrender, He completely reversed my bad attitude. I no longer had a heart that was resisting the call to home-school; I had a heart rejoicing in the call to home-school! Only God can change a heart that way!

The Lord has shown us tremendous favor in regards to our homeschooling. Immediately, I sat the boys down and talked with them about everything. They were confused and scared anyway, as they sat in the living room listening to me scream at God from my bedroom. They needed a good talking to. We began by praying together. God showed up! I cry as I write this...remembering their little faces sitting across the room from me. They listened quietly and processed what I was saying. I was expecting tears and drama of mass proportions after announcing that they'd not be returning to their school or their friends. That isn't what happened, however, and in a matter of minutes any anxiety that was there disappeared. God relieved all our fears and gave us a great sense of hope and excitement for this new adventure.

One of the major decisions that had to be considered was the ability for my kids to continue participating in sports. They are sports crazy! There was no way they were going to be happy boys without the prospects of playing organized sports. I was thrilled to find out that it was a possibility with the homeschooling laws in our state. However, my oldest son began having concerns after summer vacation our first year of homeschooling. He hadn't seen his friends, or any public school children for the duration of summer break and began fearing football sign-ups. It was as if he was the "new kid," and all of the typical anxieties that accompany being a "new kid" washed over him. Before practices started, his dad and I prayed with him and invited the Lord to have His way in my son's athletic career. So far, the Lord has demonstrated great favor on my son with each new season. He has never felt ostracized as a homeschooler. That's a big testimony in our household!

Financially, homeschooling is tough. I teach the kids full-time and that means we forego a second income. God has been faithful each year to supply for all of our schoolroom needs. This last season, I was struggling to see where the finances would come from for some of our significant curriculum choices. We are frugal and I spend extra time preparing a lot of the lessons to help save money, but there are a few choices we've made in our schooling that require money. When the time came to purchase these items, there were no funds available. I began to panic and jumped to the conclusions that maybe I had never heard from the Lord regarding the "home-school" issue. I assumed that I made up in my own mind the entire series of events that led me to home-school in the first place. Yes, there is a sad story in there...another one of those ugly recipes. That's when the Lord spoke to me using the verses heading this chapter from Colossians 2. Those verses have become the mission of our school. The reason it was so significant to me is because of a certain play on words. Remember, God speaks the language of my heart! This very scripture reference contains the phrasing of the title to the exact curriculum I needed to purchase at the time. Not coincidentally, on that same day He met our needs financially as provision for the curriculum.

There have been many sticky notes with different lists and important reminders written on them in our classroom...some of them written in crayon, some in pencil that have faded over time; and some have been written in chalk and turned to dust. Even some of the ones written in ink have smudged, or lost their stickiness and fallen behind a desk. One thing is for certain, though...today this sticky note in my hand marked with the verses from Colossians is getting framed and hung permanently on our classroom wall! Now that sounds like a recipe for success!

> *"How sweet are your words to my taste, sweeter than honey to my mouth!"*
> Psalm 119:103

12

$481.00

I was driving with my husband that night, headed out to the grocery store to pick up some essentials. On the way, we were discussing the chapters of this book. It came to our attention that these stories are NOT the significant or BIG testimonies that we would naturally tell when recalling the things the Lord has done on our behalf. There are some whoppers! He has been so good to us! However, these *little* stories have been quickened to my heart recently, one at a time, and a nudge has been placed in me to remember these seemingly smaller testimonies in this book format. As my husband inquired further into the details of some of the later chapters I've written that he's not had the chance to read, we discussed the fact that the only audience this book may ever meet is the two of us. Make that three, because I know my mama (in-law...but "who needs formalities?") will read it, too. We discussed whether or not I should finish these last couple of chapters, or whether its purpose had already been served. My own attitude has changed. The muck is NOT gone; matter of fact its seeming to get thicker in a few places, but the purpose of regaining some spiritual strength to plow on through the storm has been accomplished. I praise the Lord for that!

The reason I'm telling you about the conversation I had with my husband that night, is to shed light on the fact that while we were discussing the early termination of my writing efforts, the Lord quickened my heart to *yet another story*. That tells me He's not done walking down Victory Lane with me quite yet. I don't hear Him giving any direction in moving forward...but He's clearly with me, revisiting these places we've been. So, while these stories may not make sense to many people, God is doing a tremendous amount of work in me through them...and that is reason enough to keep going. Here goes.

The sticky note that adorns the title of this chapter reads $481.00. The sad story that prompted me to write that sum of money on a sticky note in the first place has to do with a death in the family and my sudden travels back home. There is no need to elaborate as it would defeat the purposes of these writings, and the word *death* gives a general idea of the sad story anyway. I want to mention that the sad story here is a lengthy one. If I were to write it out, I'd need several pages just to convey how my heart felt during that time. I feel the need to tell you that I clearly thought I had heard from the Lord that it was absolutely necessary to travel back to my hometown for the funeral and to be with family during this time. This seemed impossible, but I inconvenienced my family (and my landlords) by using our rent money to purchase an airline ticket. The only thing you must really know to understand the purpose of this dollar amount is that $481.00 was the exact cost of my plane ticket to suddenly travel back to my hometown to be with my extended family.

The sad story here is NOT mostly about the death of my family member. That sounds heartless, because we were of course terribly saddened at the loss; but my own heart experienced a different kind of loss during that trip - one I am not going to revisit now. I want to share with you the feelings of confusion I had, though. When I purchased the airline ticket, I was confident that the Lord told me I had to go. When I returned, heartbroken and confused, I was especially upset because it seemed I most likely had not heard clearly from the Lord. I was embarrassed to return to my family, having spent our rent money on what I thought was going to be some huge working of the Lord within my family that NEVER happened. The hour-long drive home from the airport that night gave me time to really talk with the Lord about what had happened. I didn't really hear much from the Lord, but a peace washed over me and I had no worry about the rent money, the brokenness, or the confusion I felt. I knew it was His calming influence.

As I reached the mile and a half road leading to my own home, I thanked the Lord for washing His peace over me, and closed my prayer time with a whisper..."*would you please help me pay my rent?*"

Pulling the car off to the side of the road, I rolled down the window and reached inside the mailbox to retrieve the mail I'd received during my time away. Mixed in with the usual combination of junk and bills was an odd looking letter from the hospital we had used for services when we lived in Kansas two years prior. Not expecting a bill from them, I swallowed the lump in my throat and opened it to find a check made out to me for the amount of $481.00!!!! I'm not kidding! Apparently, I had overpaid a $67.00 hospital bill by $481.00! I went back to through my check registers wondering how I could have made the mistake of writing the hospital a $548.00 check instead of a $67.00 one. After an 11-month time lapse, somehow I made one error after another that had kept my mistake concealed. After obtaining the cancelled check from my bank, the proof was there. I had actually overpaid them by $481.00 and never overdrawn my checking account! Then, after all that time, I received a refund check for the exact amount of my plane ticket the very day I returned home (having whispered a faint prayer to the Lord asking for help in recovering the monies I'd spent.)

Coincidence? I think NOT! God is so creative in the ways He plans and strategizes on our behalf. What hit me most, though, was the realization that 11 months earlier, God was working on my behalf to orchestrate all of this. I think of my usual routine when paying bills. The way I talk with Him and chit-chat about how I'm paying this or how I'm not paying that. He's there. He's **really** there working out every detail, sometimes months and I'll bet even years in advance. I think He even likes paying bills with me!

I am embarrassed to admit to you that up until the Lord quickened my heart with this story, I'd not thought of it for years. How have I let such a meaningful thing fade away? I'm so thankful that even when I've taken my eye off of Him, He never loses sight of me.

This isn't just a testimony about financial provision. That part is incredible; but it's also a testimony of how God works on our behalf before we even know we need something worked out...it's about His perfect timing. And it's about His acknowledging to me that I had in fact been obedient when I got on that plane in the first place. He was restoring my finances, my faith and my confidence that I had actually been hearing from the Lord...all in one fell swoop! WOW!

After all these years, His timing again proves perfect. Even as He reminds me of these things that happened then, I find my faith firming up now...just when I need it most. (Forget the $481.) That's what I would call...*priceless*.

13

It's a Girl

Congratulations!

After the birth of our three beautiful sons, my husband and I were blessed to have a daughter of our own. This is a twisting and turning adventure that we are only four years into. Already there have been many sad stories and scary times involving a vast array of issues. She is clearly my miracle child and the Lord has made it very certain that His hand is upon this girl! Someday, I'll tell the full story surrounding the little life inside this blonde-haired, blue-eyed beauty I'm so fond of...sad stories and all. For now, though, I'm only going to tell of a happier time.

I touched base a little bit in an earlier chapter about this longing I had for a daughter that was rooted from the absence of a healthy mother-daughter relationship as a child myself. I also talked of how the Lord began the process of restoring this relationship dynamic to me by knitting my heart with my mother-in-law's. We had been enjoying a healthy mother-daughter relationship for five years when the Lord began preparing my heart to be a mother to my own little girl.

My heart yearned for a girl for many years. Alleviated only temporarily by the occasional visits from my two nieces, I found it difficult to cope with the thought that the Lord may never give me a daughter of my own. My youngest son was now four years old. I didn't really desire my children to have large age gaps and I felt myself giving up hope. My husband and I talked openly about our fears of never having a daughter. How could something that burned so desperately inside of me be denied? As time passed and God wasn't saying "YES" to my dreams of a little girl, I assumed He was saying "NO." I began to dabble in depression a little bit, and I remember mourning over the loss of her...the loss of the hope of the dream of her. That's a mouthful! One night, however, the Lord restored my dream by waking me up!

I sat up in my bed suddenly speaking the name "Abigail" out loud. I wasn't so loud as to wake my husband, so I carefully crawled out of bed and opened my Bible. I knew there had been a woman in the Bible named Abigail. I was stirred in my spirit regarding this desire for a daughter, and I knew God was pointing me to His answer regarding whether or not I would ever have a daughter of my own. That answer would be found in the Bible wherever Abigail was found. I was soooo stirred up, and hope overwhelmed me.

One of the reasons for that overwhelming hope was the fact that I believed God was speaking to me regarding this desire for a daughter, using the name Abigail for a very specific reason. During all our years of having children, my husband and I came to the decision that if we had boys, each boy's name would start with the letter "B" in honor of his name starting with one. If we had a daughter, her name would start with an "A" in honor of my name starting with one. As the Lord woke me from my sleep stirring my heart with the name Abigail, I began to hope again, trembling with fear at the same time. I was so scared to let myself hope, fearful to be let down or to find myself in a state of mourning all over again, had I heard incorrectly. I had almost talked myself out of searching the scriptures that night for the story of Abigail, but the Holy Spirit continued to nudge me onward, until I came to **1 Samuel 25:32, "David said to Abigail, 'Praise be to the Lord, the God of Israel, who has sent you today to meet me.' "**

The Lord gave me a vision that night of myself as David, who was speaking to a little girl those very words. I began to thank Him right then and there for my very own Abigail.

Having been awake in the middle of the night with all of this, I found myself sleepy again and crawled back into bed, waking again only to find that my husband had already left for work before I had had the chance to tell him about this amazing encounter I'd had with the Lord that night!

I buzzed around the house all day, planning, preparing and rehearsing how to tell my husband what I believed the Lord was saying to us: I believed he was speaking to us through the 1 Samuel verses, where David gave thanks to the Lord for sending him Abigail. I believed he was using these verses to confirm to my heart that we would be thanking Him for our very own Abigail someday. After all that buzzing and over-thinking, I convinced myself I was nuts, and that I had fabricated the entire thing myself. Praying to the Lord, I confessed my fears and humbly asked God again for confirmation BEFORE I told my husband anything about the encounter.

(This part is amazing!)

That afternoon, I was outside with the kids at the swing set, pushing the boys on the swings. It was a beautiful day, and I expected that my husband would work late into the evening hours on the outdoor construction project where he was working, to make the most out of this favorable weather. Much to my surprise, the sliding glass door to our back yard slid open, my husband pounced out the door, landed on the deck, threw his arms open and exclaimed the name...(you guessed it)... "ABIGAIL!" I turned to look at him, my eyes stinging with tears held back and asked him what he was talking about. He said, *"I was thinking about 'A' names today on the drive home from work. If we ever have a daughter, what do ya' think about the name Abigail?"* I wept freely before the Lord as I shared my Abigail encounter with my husband. I don't know that he would have believed me, had I not been a faithful journal-keeper and showed him the very pages I'd penned earlier that detailed everything. (Journal-keeping **does** pay off, but that's another story.)

Finally I believed I had the answer to my prayers. Now we wanted to know *when...*

After a few sad stories challenged my faith in the promise I believed God had spoken, I remember lying on the specialist's cold exam table at 16 weeks pregnant. When the doctor squirted my belly with jelly, He turned the sonogram screen so I could see my baby for the first time. My early pregnancy had seen some pretty serious complications. As such, I was considered a high-risk pregnancy and was now required to frequent a specialist for regular sonograms. At 16 weeks pregnant, I hadn't thought twice about knowing the sex of the baby, remembering from previous pregnancies that gender usually wasn't seen until about 20 weeks gestation. The doctor continued his exam and then casually inquired, "Want to know the sex of the baby? I can tell you."

My body froze, but my mind panicked, racing with what seemed like a zillion "what-ifs." On top of it all, I was in the exam room alone with no one to comfort me should this doctor tell me I was having a boy, and I would realize that all the time I spent believing the Lord for my own Abigail was a lie. My husband was down in the car with all my sons who had fallen asleep during the hour long car ride to this appointment, so I took a deep breath and said to myself, "*Here we go, Lord.*"

Once the doctor confirmed I was having a daughter, I cried uncontrollably and the nurse had to explain to him the reason for such dramatics. "She has three sons," the nurse alerted him. He immediately began to back track a little with statistics of sonograms not being 100% accurate, nervously covering his own tracks just in case he'd gotten my hopes up mistakenly. Even so I left, having been cited the doctor's credentials by the nurses. And they even tooted his horn for having never been wrong in reading a baby's gender in all his years as a specialist!

I ran to the car to tell my husband and he had just as much trouble believing it at first as I did. My husband's parents however, went out and bought something pink that very day.

Though finding out the gender of your promised daughter at only 16 weeks gestation is really amazing and wonderful, it's a really long time to wait until you KNOW FOR SURE. I struggled with doubt from time to time, but found comfort in the Lord's "Abigail" Word spoken to me out of 1 Samuel. I referred to it often. That, coupled with the enjoyment I got out of buying everything pink in sight (retail therapy?) got me through all those remaining weeks of waiting.

I can't leave this chapter without telling you about the moment my girl arrived, which happened to be the moment God completed the healing process of my heart. No longer did I have a hole in my heart where "mother" or "daughter" belonged. Her grand entrance came three weeks early as my body could barely contain her 10 lb. 01 oz. frame any longer.

My obstetrician happened to be the same doctor who delivered my third son. I had shared with her the details of the Lord's promise that this would be my daughter during our routine visits. As the first witness to my promise-come-true, she tore down the blue curtain hanging as a divider between my head and my C-sectioned abdomen, held a very fat baby with its legs spread open in front of my face and wildly exclaimed, "Look at her beautiful vagina!" The room burst at the seams with laughter and tears as everyone in the room beheld something very special that the Lord did that day. Rejoicing went forth as I lifted this prayer to heaven: **"Praise be to the Lord, the God of Israel, who has sent you today to meet me..."**

In case you're wondering...my husband and I hold the name 'Abigail' very near to our hearts; however, we chose NOT to actually name our daughter with that name because of the fact that two of our extended family's pet dogs donned the name. After prayer, we feel the Lord gave us the perfect alternative 'A' name.

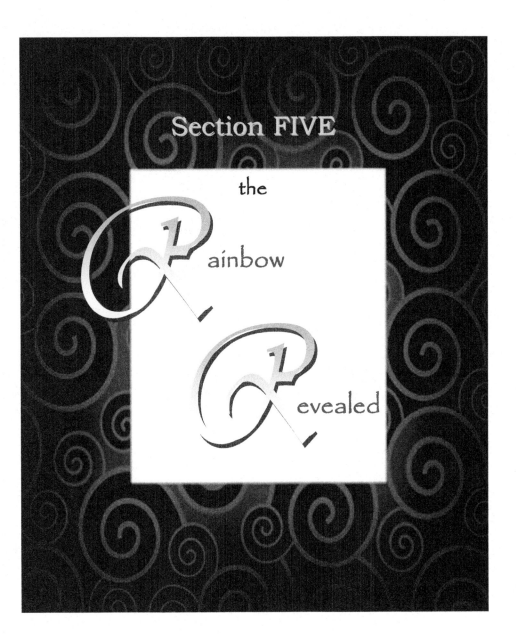

Section FIVE

the

Rainbow

Revealed

14

Colored Index Cards

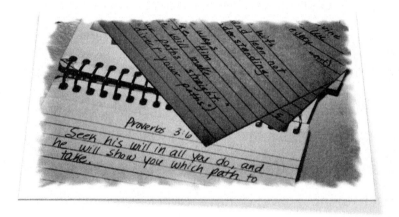

This process of walking with the Lord back down my own Victory Lane has been life-changing for me! He has helped me visit the once muck-filled potholes, and He has repaved them for me...strengthening various vital aspects of my hope and faith. The stories and testimonies I've encountered in these past places of my life were ones that I'd forgotten. Not the "big testimonies" I thought I'd be writing about, but the ones less remembered have proved to be the ones having a greater impact on me. I'm reminded of the verse in 1 Corinthians 1:27 (KJV) where it says, **"...but God hath chosen the foolish things of the world to confound the wise..."** I realize that none of the blessings or workings on our behalf from the Lord are actually weak, but as we tend to weigh everything on a scale (think "from 1 to 10"), these testimonies and memories of times past have not been what I would have considered my "heavy hitters." Yet, those "heavy hitters" couldn't lift my eyes; couldn't restore my joy; couldn't firm up my faith, hope or trust in the Lord during this current season of rough weather I'd been experiencing. God knew that I needed to go backward to see Him with a fresh perspective of how He's worked throughout my life. I'm finding that the Lord tends to do a lot of things in a way that I would coin as "**backwards**," only to prove to me that His methods are always purposeful to get me going in the right direction; and that direction is always **back** to HIM.

Throughout this book, I have referred to these little reminders as sticky notes. Remember back to the beginning of the book with me, where I metaphorically told of the need to redecorate the walls of my heart and the dusty corners of my mind with sticky note reminders – the ones that had lost their stickiness over time. I have purposed to take down the sad stories that once hung on display for all to see. However, when I began this chapter of the book, knowing it would be my last chapter, I decided to divert from the usual detours around the sad stories.

It's not a sad story in the typical sense conveyed by the word "sad." The only way it is sad is by the way this story was marked with my disobedient, stubborn, selfish and rebellious heart. (Not so long ago.)

Let's go back to the beginning of this chapter. I've titled it **Colored Index Cards** for a reason. Just under a year ago, as I took part in a prayer movement at my church, I picked up a tip from a friend to start writing reference scriptures on spiral-bound colored index cards to keep with me at all times. It was smaller than a Bible, and the scriptures written on them were my "life verses," the very scriptures from which I drew the resources necessary for life; not only for myself, but also for others. Many times throughout the year, these scriptures seemed to have been hand-chosen by God Himself for the different situations and encounters I'd faced. Clearly He was using them for my good and the good of others around me. I took notice that more women from my church were also carrying their own stack...it was like a *colored index card* *movement!* It's kind of funny, actually. What isn't funny, however, is the fact that two months ago I made a choice to remove the colored index cards from my purse and to place them up high on a shelf in my closet.

You see, something rather significant happened in my life two months ago that has been ongoing since then, and it makes up a hefty portion of the muck I've been stuck in. I wasn't hearing from the Lord regarding this situation, really. I especially wasn't getting any new scriptures for my cards. (To be perfectly honest, there may have been some, but my heart didn't want to see them or apply them – so I may have ignored them.) You might say I threw a hissy fit. Pouting was definitely involved, as was anger and rebellion. The thought behind the action of removing the colored index cards from my purse was two-fold. First, I thought it might finally get God's attention. After all, if I wasn't hearing from the Lord, He must've just overlooked me. This would make Him take notice! Secondly, I assumed that getting no answer from the Lord automatically meant that the answer was "no," when I wanted a "yes" answer. I don't typically enjoy being told "no." So, I figured that if I set aside the colored index cards in which He usually communicates with me, then I'd be protecting myself from hearing something I may not actually want to hear. It was a stupid move.

A funny memory my mother-in-law shared with me recently comes to mind as I write this. She was recalling some arguments she'd had with her sisters as a child. When she'd grown tired of yelling out *her side of the story,* and didn't want to hear theirs...she'd close her eyes and put her hands over her ears. She said she might have even stood in another part of the room. And then she would make a loud nonsense noise like "laa, laa, laa...I can't heeeeear you," until her sisters got tired and gave the issue a rest. We agreed that was pretty childish and stupid too!

Back into my life now, without having those life verses at hand, I quickly began a downward spiral deeper and deeper into my mucky puddle. I not only didn't have the resources I needed to get through my own life, but I no longer had the resources necessary to be a good friend to anyone else. If I don't have the living truth of God's Word at my fingertips, then what do I have ?!?

Sometime last week, in the process of writing this book, my perspective really did begin to change. And I see now that my faith is strengthened; my hope is renewed; and I have found rest and peace in trusting God's plans. I have also seen my own sin during these last two months' time, and have had to come before the Lord with a repentant heart.

At about that same time, I began experiencing little tugs at my heart strings, feelings that made me think I should pull out my colored index cards again and put them back into my purse. I was embarrassed to do it, though. I knew I had made a mistake by casting them aside in the first place, and I felt the enemy was trying to place shame on me about being rebellious with the Lord. This dastardly pair of nagging thoughts worked together to make it a very difficult task to move the cards back into my purse. I found myself delaying the process, and assuming that colored index cards with scriptures written on them really couldn't mean all that much to the Lord.

Then one day last week, my mother-in-law called me and we chatted about Christmas plans and different things. We didn't chat long, as I was distracted because I was preparing to wrap presents with the kids with the intention of baking Christmas cookies afterward. Just before hanging up, she said to me, "Oh! I forgot to tell you. I felt the Lord wanted me to buy colored index cards at the dollar store the other day and write down some important scriptures for you to have; I'll bring them over."

WOW.

She did not know anything about my little colored cards or the way God had been working on my heart regarding them. Such a seemingly small thing to her has ended up speaking volumes to me.

My Mom was faithful to write down the scriptures she felt the Lord wanted me to have. I added them to the spiral-bound colored index cards I retrieved from the shelf in my closet...and placed them back in my purse where they belong. (I could almost hear the angels clapping.) God even spoke to me out of Psalm 119:100-115 immediately upon their retrieval. I am currently using the New Living Translation for my own personal Bible, and in it He especially highlighted these following verses:

> *v. 103 – "How sweet your words taste to me; they are sweeter than honey."*
>
> *v. 105 – "Your word is a lamp to guide my feet and a light for my path."*
>
> *v. 107 – "I have suffered much, O Lord; restore my life again as you promised."*
>
> *v. 109 – "My life constantly hangs in the balance, but I will not stop obeying your instructions."*
>
> *v. 114 – "You are my refuge and my shield; your Word is my source of hope."*

This journey through the sticky notes of my past has been an amazing one...but I can't wait to one day visit the colored index cards of my future! *Hallelujah!*

~~~~~~~~~~~~~~~~~~~~~~~~~~~~~~

THE END???

Traveling backwards to get to the beginning of my walk with the Lord; only to have it bring me back to the end so I could have a new beginning or...um...er...uh...wait! I'm confused!?!

Beginning or End – it has always been GOD.

And just as we began our journey (see Introduction) off on the right foot, stepping on the truth of God's Word in Revelation 21; I believe it would be appropriate to end our journey there as well, feet firmly planted.

Beginning or End – it has always been GOD.

> "He will wipe every tear from their eyes. There will be no more death or mourning or crying or pain for the old order of things has passed away." He who was seated on the throne said, "I am making everything new!" Then He said, "Write this down, for these words are trustworthy and true." He said to me: "It is done. I am the Alpha and the Omega, the Beginning and the End..."
> **Revelation 21:4-6**

ABOUT THE AUTHOR

 Amber Dobson Woodrum is a "thirty-something" wife and mother of four children. She currently resides in the state of Washington where she home-schools her children and enjoys taking road trips to the ocean and mountains with her family. Her favorite past-times are freelance photography, writing and watching her children play sports. She and her husband will be celebrating their 15th Wedding Anniversary this year.

Amber has been purposing to walk with the Lord in life since 2001, during which time she has served in many different capacities within her church including: worship teams, nursery school teacher, ministry teams, planning committees, leadership roles and Financial Treasurer.

Look for more titles available from Amber Dobson Woodrum.

CPSIA information can be obtained at www.ICGtesting.com
Printed in the USA
BVOW05s2307130916

462014BV00023B/248/P